Polymer Clay Basics

Welcome to Art Faces in Clay ! Get ready to have a great time !!

Condition clay: Warm and knead clay until smooth and elastic. The kneading process strengthens the clay. • If clay is stiff, mix in a softer clay or add liquid Clay Softener (diluent) by Polyform or Mix Quick Kneading Medium by Eberhard Faber.

Safety: (1) Don't eat it. Keep all clay tools separate from those used for food. Once used for clay, don't use it again for food. (2) Don't burn it. Use a timer, test oven with a separate thermometer for accuracy, and bake in the center of the oven for even heating.

Baking: For the strongest end product, bake at the highest temperature and the longest time listed on the package. Generally this is 265°-275°F for 30 minutes or 30 minutes per 1/4" of thickness. Some brands of clay scorch easily. It is best to build thick pieces over an aluminum foil armature.

Gluing: Test the glue that you are using to be sure that it will hold its bond on polymer clay. Many will not. I use *Super Glue* to bond jewelry findings, and *Crafter's Pick* The Ultimate! to bond baked polymer to other surfaces such as paper and cloth. *Beacon* Fabri-Tac works well as a quick bond for yarn hair. When bonding unbaked clay to baked clay, use a thin coating of liquid polymer clay.

Materials for use in the molds: Most of the faces included in this book were made with Polymer Clay, which is an oven baked clay. However, many of the designs could also be done using an air-dry or paper clay. Since the molds are flexible, a material that hardens in the mold, such as Ultra Thick Embossing Enamel, could also be used. Be sure to coat the mold with a release agent such as clear embossing ink, when using UTEE. Other materials that may be used are plaster and wax.

Bendi Doll instructions on page 21.

Using Designer Push Molds for Flat Images

1. Roll conditioned polymer clay into a smooth ball.

2. Roll ball into basic shape of mold cavity. Flatten slightly.

3. Press clay into mold.

4. Press away from edge, toward center, so entire edge is visible. Trim away excess.

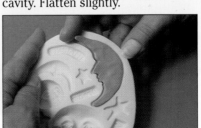

5. Flex mold slightly and lift image.

6. Lay the molded image on your work surface. It is ready to alter, shape and decorate.

Altering Molded Faces

Here's where you can have some major fun!

Squeeze, pinch, reshape and cut. You will be surprised at how many different faces you will be able to get from these easy-to-use push molds.

Have a contest with your family to see how many looks you really can get. Have fun!

Compressing

1. The two small Sun faces shown above started out the same.

2. To alter the face, push the opposite sides of the face together to compress.

Changing the Shape

1. These 2 moon faces started out the same. The ends were pinched off, then reshaped, as was the nose.

Cutting

1. This Moon face was molded, then cut apart. This works best if the image is flat, so don't overfill the mold.

Using Part of a Mold

1. These faces were all made from the same original face from the Tribal Mold.

2. Fill just part of the mold. Experiment!

Using Deeper Molds

1. Brush mold with cornstarch or baby powder. Shake out excess until no powder is visible. Follow basic steps 1 - 5.

2. Press a wad of soft clay to the back of the trimmed image. Lift image straight out of mold.

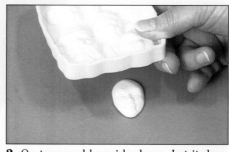

3. Or, turn mold upside down. Let it drop from mold.

Here's a great little project to get you started!

1. Sponge and layer paint:
Use a damp sponge and very little paint to build up layers of color. Add opaque paints in any order. Start with the lightest shades of translucents.

2. Diamond Glaze:
Drizzle Diamond Glaze on the desired area. Sprinkle beads. Let dry. Shake off the excess beads.

3. Painted dots:
Dip a knitting needle into a puddle of paint. Tap lightly on surface.

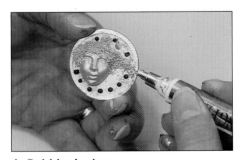

4. Gold leaf edge:
Apply the Krylon marker to both the paper and clay.

Circle Tags

Use these decorative tags on bookmarks, scrapbook pages, cards, gift tags and altered art. You will love the sparkle these unique pieces add to every project.

Silver Wind
MATERIALS: *AMACO* (Victorian Push Mold; Any color polymer clay) • Metal rimmed tag • *Krylon* Gold Leafing pen • *Lumiere* paint (Metallic Gold, Super Bronze, Pearl Violet) • *Kreinik* metallic ribbon • Silver glass micro beads • *JudiKins* Diamond Glaze • Sponge • *The Ultimate!* glue
INSTRUCTIONS: Use part of face to make medium Victorian face. • Bake and paint. • Glue face to tag. Drizzle on Diamond Glaze. Add beads. • Dot on paint, starting with large dots. Let dry. • Add second layer of smaller dots. • Add ribbon.

Mysterious Face
MATERIALS: *AMACO* (Victorian Push Mold; Any color polymer clay) • Metal rimmed tag • *Lumiere* paint (Metallic Gold, Super Bronze, Pearl Violet) • *Kreinik* Silk Bella thread • Silver glass micro beads • *JudiKins* Diamond Glaze • Sponge • *The Ultimate!* glue
INSTRUCTIONS: Make face from Victorian mold. Trim. • Bake and paint. • Sponge tag. • Glue face to card. Drizzle on Diamond Glaze. Add beads. • Dot rim with paint. Add thread.

Altering Molded Faces

Try out these terrific techniques to bring your projects to life.

Remember the more you do the better you get!

Stretching

1. These two small Suns are different sizes due to stretching.

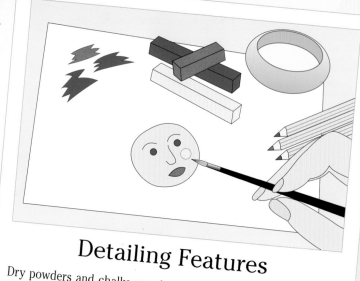

Detailing Features

Dry powders and chalks may be applied to unbaked face with a tiny brush to "paint" features. Details can also be added after baking face. For tips, see Painted Faces #1.

2. Carefully stretch all edges, then smooth with finger.

Change Expression

Add Detail

1. Give the Sun a smiling face by pressing IN at the corners

1. Add detail to faces using a clay shaper.

Close Eyes

1. Some faces are easy to change.

2. Then press up.

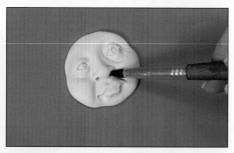

2. Use a clay shaper to lift nostrils.

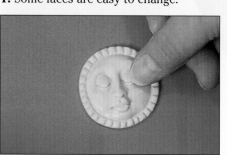

2. Gently pat and smooth the eye closed.

3. Smooth brow upwards to relax eyebrow area.

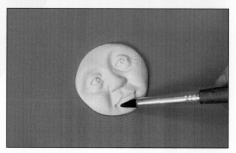

3. Roll the tool under the mouth to make the lips more pronounced.

Embellishing Molded Faces

Painted Faces

1. What Paints to Use: Acrylic paint may completely mask the color of clay. You can also use Genesis Heat Set Artist Oils and watercolor paint. Watercolor paint must be sealed with a spray sealer, such as Duncan Super Matte Ceramic Sealer or Duncan Porcelain Spray. Be careful when applying spray sealers, as many will not dry on polymer clay, but will turn sticky.

2. Bake face. Cool. Apply paint.

Applying Dry Powders

1. Before baking, while clay is still sticky, brush on dry powders such as Pearl-Ex, powdered makeup or chalk.

2. Brush firmly for maximum adhesion. The color of the clay may show through the powders.

Antiquing

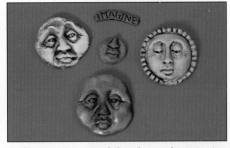

1. Change the tint of the clay with antiquing techniques.

2. Paint face with acrylic paint darker than clay. Burnt Umber or a softer Brown work well. Wipe off immediately. If antiquing is too light, reapply. Use a damp brush to remove excess paint from crevices. If you are unhappy with the results, and it won't wash off, use a toothbrush and scrub!

Mixing It Up... Creating Faux Finishes

Faux Marble Clay

1. Mix and fold together translucent, White and earth-colored clays. Experiment with color combinations. Often leftover clays in a pile yield the best mixes!

Faux Jade Clay

1. Mix together 1/4 block of translucent clay with a tiny pea-sized piece of Leaf Green clay. For color variation, add a mustard seed amount of Violet clay. Do not mix the clay completely. Smudge colors across the surface to create veins of color. Clay may appear pale until after baking, when color will show through the translucent mix. Test bake a piece if you are concerned about the exact color.

Faux Ivory Clay

1. Mix together 1 part White and 1 part Ivory or Champagne to get a Pale Ivory color. Roll this into a long log. Roll a second log of translucent clay alongside the pale Ivory log. Cut the two logs into sections. Stack. Roll into a log shape. Cut, stack and repeat until clay has a fine grain line. Use a section of this mix in the mold.

Embellished Playing Cards

Turn ordinary playing cards into an extraordinary work of art. Frame them together to decorate your game room, or mount them on sticks for an interesting table centerpiece.

2 of Spades
MATERIALS: *AMACO* (Tribal Push Mold; Gold polymer clay) • Playing card • *Lumiere* paint (Metallic Gold, Super Copper) • Gold metallic braid • Purple glass micro beads • *JudiKins* Diamond Glaze • 1/8" hole punch • Sponge • *The Ultimate!* glue • Glitter glue
INSTRUCTIONS: Make and bake face, using just part of the mold. • Sponge card with Lumiere paint. • Punch holes in card. Stitch with Gold braid. • Glue face to card. • Drizzle Diamond Glaze on card. Sprinkle on beads. Dot with glitter glue.

Queen of Clubs
MATERIALS: *AMACO* (Victorian Push Mold; Pale Beige polymer clay) • Playing card • *Krylon* Gold Leafing pen • *Lumiere* paint (Metallic Gold, Metallic Olive Green) • *Kreinik* Green 1/16" metallic ribbon • 1/8" hole punch • Sponge • *The Ultimate!* glue
INSTRUCTIONS: Make and bake 2 small faces from Victorian mold. • Paint clay and sponge card. • Embellish card with Gold leafing pen. • Punch holes in card. Add stitching. • Glue faces to card. • Add paint dots with knitting needle. See photo.

10 of Clubs
MATERIALS: *AMACO* (Sun Push Mold; Any color polymer clay) • Playing card • *Lumiere* paint (Metallic Gold, Pearl Violet, Super Copper) • *Kreinik* (1/8" Lilac metallic ribbon, Silk Bella thread) • 1/8" hole punch • Sponge • *The Ultimate!* glue
INSTRUCTIONS: Make face from Sun mold, stretching to elongate. Bake. • Paint face. • Sponge card with Lumiere paint. • Punch holes in card. Add stitching. • Glue face to card.

are Great Fun!
Make them All!

Ace of Hearts

MATERIALS: *AMACO* (Push Molds: Victorian, Moon; Any color polymer clay) • Playing card • 3 puzzle pieces • *Lumiere* paint (Metallic Gold, Pearl Violet) • *Kreinik* 1/8" metallic ribbon (Lilac, Gold) • Glass micro beads (Purple, Gold, Silver) • *JudiKins* Diamond Glaze • 1/8" hole punch • Sponge • *The Ultimate!* glue

INSTRUCTIONS: Use part of the face from Victorian mold and the word Dream from the Moon mold. Bake clay. • Paint clay and puzzle pieces. • Sponge card with Gold paint. • Punch holes in card and add stitching. • Glue pieces to card. Add Lilac ribbon across puzzle pieces. Glue ends to back of card. • Drizzle on Diamond Glaze and add beads, 1 color at a time. Let set between colors.

Making Monoprints

1. Dab the acrylic paint onto the playing card.

2. Press another card on top.

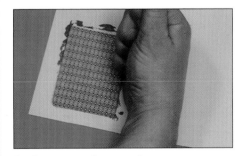

3. Pull apart.

Mini Envelopes
become part of your art

These pretty envelopes hold fun clay art pieces. Use them as bookmarks, or add a magnet and brighten a refrigerator door or metal cabinet. Attach the Rising Sun to your computer monitor to bring some "light" into your work day.

The Rising Sun
MATERIALS: *AMACO* (Sun Push Mold; Polymer clay: Yellow, White) • 2" x 3" envelope • *Lumiere* paint (Pearl Blue, Gold) • Cream cardstock • *Kreinik* 1/8" Lilac metallic ribbon • *Krylon* Gold Leafing Pen • Sponge • *The Ultimate!* glue

INSTRUCTIONS: Mix clay to make Pale Yellow. • Make and bake sun face and the word "Light". • Antique face. Paint word Pearl Blue. Apply a light coat of Gold paint to sun. • Cut cardstock to fit envelope. Glue face to cardstock. • Sponge envelope with Pearl Blue paint. • Edge envelope and word with Gold pen. • Glue embellishments to envelope.

Basic Embellishment Techniques for Paper and Clay
While most of these techniques are shown using paper, many can be used on polymer clay. Think of polymer clay as a surface, ready to explore with paints, stamps, and inks. The effect will vary for baked and nonbaked clay.

Inked Edge

1. Tap or drag ink pad along edge of paper and baked or unbaked clay.

Stamped Words

1. Leather stamps make deeply etched lettering into unbaked clay.

Imagine
MATERIALS: *AMACO* (Tribal Push Mold; Polymer clay: Brown, Gold, Copper, Champagne) • 2" x 3" envelope • *Lumiere* paint (Super Copper, Metallic Bronze, Pearl Violet) • Burnt Umber acrylic paint • *Kreinik* Lilac metallic thread • *The Leather Factory* Alphabet Stamps #8137 • *The Ultimate!* glue

INSTRUCTIONS: Roll 2 strips of Champagne clay 1" x 2". Press into the words Spirit and Legend in mold. Trim to fit into envelope. • Make tribal faces from mold and press to clay strips. • Use leather stamps to imprint word "Imagine". Poke holes on both sides of word "Imagine". • Bake clay, then antique. • Sand top of words to reveal light clay color. • Sponge envelope with Lumiere paint. • Thread ribbon through "Imagine" and tie around envelope.

Stippled Edge

1. Pounce a stiff, nearly dry brush on surface.

Curled Wire

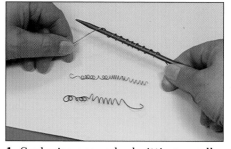

1. Curl wire around a knitting needle, skewer, or paint brush handle, then stretch or flatten for a different look.

Gift Tags

These tags are so much fun, you won't be able to decide which one to do first, and then you won't want to quit making them! Everyone on your list will want one of these expressive art tags.

Using Just Part of a Mold

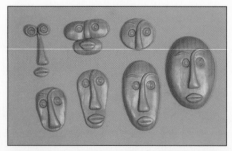

1. These faces were all made from the same original face from the Tribal Mold.

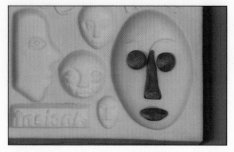

2. Fill just part of the mold. Experiment!

to top off that special gift

Myth Tag
MATERIALS: *AMACO* (Push Molds: Moon, Tribal; Ivory polymer clay; *WireForm* Brass Decorative Mesh) • Shipping tag • *Lumiere* Metallic Olive Green paint • Purple acrylic paint • String • Green *Kreinik* metallic thread • Green paper • Sponge • *The Ultimate!* glue
INSTRUCTIONS: Make a large moon face and the word "myth" from clay. Trim face. • Bake clay. • Antique clay. • Sponge shipping tag with Lumiere. Paint string and word "myth" Purple. • Tear Green paper to fit across length of tag. Layer tag, paper, mesh, and face. Glue pieces in place. • Add fibers.

Wish Tag
MATERIALS: *AMACO* (Push Molds: Sun, Moon; Gold polymer clay) • Tags (1 metal rimmed, 1 shipping) • *Lumiere* paint (Metallic Gold, Metallic Olive Green) • Acrylic paint (Burnt Umber, Purple) • Gold Pearl Ex pigments • *Krylon* Gold Leafing pen • *Kreinik* Aquamarine 1/8" metallic ribbon • Dark Green paper • Sponge • *The Ultimate!* glue
INSTRUCTIONS: Make a very flat, medium sun face and the word "wish" from clay. • Brush face with Pearl-Ex powder. • Bake and antique. • Sponge paint shipping tag with Gold and Purple, round tag with Green. Edge round tag with Gold pen. • Glue pieces in place. • Add ribbon.

It's Theatre!
MATERIALS: *AMACO* (Push Molds: Victorian, Sun; Any color polymer clay) • Tags (2 metal rimmed, 1 shipping) • *Lumiere* paint (Metallic Gold, Super Bronze, Metallic Silver, Pearl Violet) • *Kreinik* metallic ribbon • Silver micro beads • *JudiKins* Diamond Glaze • Sponge • *The Ultimate!* glue
INSTRUCTIONS: Make large Victorian face and medium sun face from clay. Trim. • Bake and paint. • Sponge paint on tags. • Glue faces to round tags. Glue to shipping tag. • Drizzle on Diamond Glaze. Add beads. • Dot on paint. • Add ribbon.

Spirit Tag
MATERIALS: *AMACO* (Tribal Push Mold; Marbled polymer clay; *WireForm* Copper Decorative Mesh) • Shipping tag • *Lumiere* Metallic Gold paint • Burnt Umber acrylic paint • Brown ink pad • 24 gauge Copper wire • Blue yarn • Dark Green paper • Sponge • *The Ultimate!* glue
INSTRUCTIONS: Make a marbled Tribal face and the word "spirit" from clay. • Bake and antique. • Add a wash of Gold paint to word. • Edge shipping tag with Brown ink. • Layer tag, paper, and face. Glue pieces together. • Curl wire. • Cut Copper mesh larger than tag. Attach mesh behind tag with yarn. Add curled wire.

Imagine Tag
MATERIALS: *AMACO* (Push Molds: Tribal, Moon; Gold polymer clay) • Tags (1 metal rimmed, 1 shipping) • *Lumiere* paint (Metallic Gold, Pearl Blue) • Burnt Umber acrylic paint • *Krylon* Gold Leafing pen • *The Leather Factory* alphabet stamps #8137 • 1/8" heart punch • String • Sponge • *The Ultimate!* glue
INSTRUCTIONS: Make a very flat, medium Tribal face and a star from clay. • Cut a narrow strip of clay to fit the bottom of the shipping tag and stamp it with word "imagine". • Bake. • Antique face and word. • Edge round tag and star with Gold pen. Sponge paint round tag. Edge shipping tag with Burnt Umber • Glue the pieces in place. • Punch hearts along bottom of shipping tag. Add string.

Tribal Mask
MATERIALS: *AMACO* (Tribal Push Mold; Copper polymer clay) • Shipping tag • *Lumiere* paint (Metallic Gold, Pearl Blue, Pearl Violet) • *Kreinik* metallic thread • Purple *Artistic Wire* 26 gauge • Sponge • *The Ultimate!* glue
INSTRUCTIONS: Use clay to make large Tribal face, using only deepest parts. Bake. • Paint. • Sponge shipping tag with Gold, Violet and Blue paint. • Glue pieces in place. • Curl wire. Attach with metallic thread.

Slide Mount Tags

These mounts are wonderful embellishments for journals, cards, and scrapbook pages. Add a bit of double-stick tape and adhere one or more to your computer monitor. For a quick gift, glue one of these mounts to a bookmark.

embellishments for scrapbook pages, cards, journals and whatever else your heart desires

Wonder
MATERIALS: *Design Originals* (Collage Paper #0551 Legacy Words; Mount #0988 Small White) • *AMACO* (Tribal Push Mold; Any color polymer clay) • *Artistic Wire* 26 gauge (Copper, Teal) • *Lumiere* paint (Pearl Blue, Pearl Violet, Metallic Gold) • Sponge • Drill • 1/8" drill bit • *The Ultimate!* glue
INSTRUCTIONS: Make 2 Tribal clay faces: one full, one partial face. • Bake and paint. • Sponge paint mount. • Curl wire. • Drill a tiny hole in the corner of the mount for attaching wire. • Glue all parts in place.

Love Poetry
MATERIALS: *Design Originals* (Collage Paper #0552 Travels; Mount #0988 Small White) • *AMACO* (Push Molds: Sun,Victorian; Polymer clay: Gold, White) • *Lumiere* paint (Metallic Gold, Super Bronze, Metallic Olive Green) • *Kreinik* Green metallic ribbon • String • *Krylon* Gold Leafing pen • Sponge • *The Ultimate!* glue
INSTRUCTIONS: Make a small, concave sun mask from White clay by not filling mold and by leaving thumb indentation in back of face. Poke 2 holes in mask for string. • Make words from Gold clay. • Bake clay. • Sponge paint mount and words. Edge mount and letters with Gold pen. • Attach string to mask. Tie bow in ribbon. • Cut picture to fit mount. • Glue all parts in place.

Dream
MATERIALS: *Design Originals* Mount #0988 Small White • *AMACO* (Moon Push Mold; Polymer clay: White, Yellow) • *Lumiere* paint (Metallic Gold, Pearl Blue) • *The Leather Factory* Alphabet Stamps #8137 • *Krylon* Gold Leafing pen • Sponge • *The Ultimate!* glue • Photograph
INSTRUCTIONS: Make a small moon face from White clay. Make the word "Dream" and a flat strip to fit side of mount from Yellow clay. • Use stamps to press the larger word "Dream" into clay strip. • Alter moon face by trimming away points and repositioning. • Bake clay. • Paint. • Sponge mount. • Glue all parts in place.

Aspire
MATERIALS: *Design Originals* (Collage Paper #0551 Legacy Words; Mount #0988 Small White) • *AMACO* (Victorian Push Mold; Gold polymer clay) • *Lumiere* paint (Super Bronze, Metallic Copper) • *Krylon* Gold Leafing pen • Sponge • *The Ultimate!* glue
INSTRUCTIONS: Make 2 large Victorian partial faces from Gold clay. • Bake and paint. • Sponge paint mount. Paint mount edge and window edge with Gold pen. • Glue all parts in place.

DREAM

BELIEVE

DREAM

BELIEVE

IMAGINE

in possibilities.

DREAM

WISH

BELIEVE

WISH Dream

Sunshine
...the light
of my life.

...and the courage
to make
your
dreams
visible.

To imagine...

You
are
the song
in my heart...

Folded
Cards

Continued on pages
16 and 17.

Art Faces In Clay 15

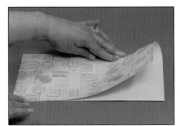

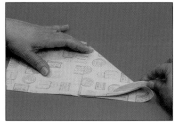

How To Fold the Card

1. Fold 12" x 12" paper in half.

2. Fold paper in half again. Use bone folder or flat tool to smooth fold.

3. Open paper to position in #1. Place paper with folded edge at top. Bring top right corner to the bottom center. Smooth fold.

4. Bring far right pointed corner to the center along bottom line. Smooth fold.

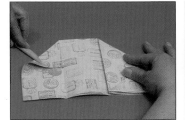

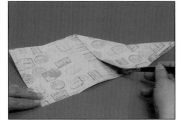

5. Bring left edge to center line. Smooth fold. Open fold. Turn top left corner down to meet folded line. Smooth fold.

6. Open card to size in picture #1. Glue 2 sides together.

7. Glue fold made in #3. Leave other folds unglued.

8. Stamp as desired.

Using MagicStamp Moldable Foam Stamp

1. Make the face using a push mold and polymer clay. Bake. Heat MagicStamp with heat gun (300°-400°F) for about 30 seconds, keeping heat gun in motion to prevent overheating. Immediately press the heated foam firmly over face for 15 - 20 seconds.

2. Let cool. Use it as a rubber stamp. If the first image doesn't turn out, reheat to create a new image.

If you have been looking for a card with an unusual fold, these are the cards for you! The folding pattern creates 5 different surfaces for you to decorate. Place the heavy clay forms on the front, while the thinner clay figures are perfect to embellish the interior pages. You will enjoy using the MagicStamp moldable foam stamp to create complementary stamps to match your clay figures.

Continued from pages 14 and 15.

Folded Cards

Dream Card
MATERIALS: *Design Originals* (Collage Paper: #0551 Legacy Words, #0548 Passport, #0483 Teal Floral; Mount #0988 Small White) • *AMACO* (Push Molds: Sun, Moon; Polymer clay: Yellow, White) • Cream cardstock • 18" Blue 1/8" suede lace • *MagicStamp* Moldable Foam Stamp • Black inkpad • *Lumiere* paint (Pearl Blue, Pearl Violet, Metallic Gold) • White acrylic paint • Sponge • *The Ultimate!* glue

Imagine Card
MATERIALS: *Design Originals* (Collage Paper: #0500 TeaDye Keys, #0544 Bingo, #0547 Dictionary, #0551 Legacy Words) • *AMACO* (Push Molds: Tribal, Moon; Copper polymer clay) • Cream cardstock • Gold micro beads • Decorated Tribal tag (see p. 6) • Decorative metal clip • *Kreinik* Lilac metallic ribbon • *MagicStamp* Moldable Foam Stamp • Black inkpad • *Lumiere* paint (Pearl Blue, Pearl Violet, Metallic Gold) • White acrylic paint • *JudiKins* Diamond Glaze • Sponge • *The Ultimate!* glue

Sunshine Card
MATERIALS: *Design Originals* Collage Paper (#0491 Coffee Stripe, #0499 TeaDye Music) • *AMACO* (Sun Push Mold; Gold polymer clay) • Cream cardstock • 18" Gold 1/8" suede lace • *Kreinik* Copper metallic thread • *MagicStamp* Moldable Foam Stamp • Black inkpad • *Lumiere* paint (Metallic Gold, Metallic Olive Green, Pearl White) • White acrylic paint • Sponge • *The Ultimate!* glue

Tips for Embellishing Cards

1. Create face and any clay embellishments from polymer clay. Poke holes in clay if piece is to be strung. Bake. Paint or antique.

2. On back of card and on collage papers for envelope, stamp image made with clay face and MagicStamp Moldable Foam Stamp.

3. Print words onto cardstock. Tear or cut out words. Layer words with torn pieces of collage papers on both card and envelope.

4. Embellish papers with sponge painting, stippling, or dotting. If paint gets too dark, sponge White or a pale color over top. Glue papers to card.

5. Glue or tie face and any other trims in place. Diamond Glaze works well for adhering tiny beads.

Dolls with Cloth Bodies
you focus on the fun part - decorating them!

These 12" Wild Woman cloth dolls from One and Only Creations come with already stuffed patterned cloth bodies, so you can focus on the fun part - decorating them! Hair fibers and faces create attitude. These dolls are really fun to embellish with wire, clay beads or ribbons.

Tip for Doll Hair: Use *FabriTac* glue to hold hair in place. Keep fingers and tools wet so the glue will not stick to you or your tools. *Fabri-Tac* grabs almost instantly to hold hair in place without a long drying time.

GENERAL MATERIALS: *One & Only Creations* 12" Wild Woman doll • Cardboard for making pom poms • Make-up blush, chalk or Pearl-Ex for cheeks • Burnt Umber or Gold paint for antiquing face • Scissors • Hemostat • Needle • Thread • *Fabri-Tac* • *The Ultimate!* (for gluing face to cloth head)

Making the Face

1. Use a push mold to make a clay face. The face fits best on the cloth head if it is concave. See below. Paint or antique the face as desired before sewing or gluing face to the cloth head.

Rose Doll
MATERIALS: *AMACO* (Victorian Push Mold; Butterfly Slice'n Bake polymer clay designs; Ivory mix polymer clay for face: White, Champagne, Transparent; Polymer Clay Blade) • *Fibers By The Yard* Pretty in Pink yarn for hair • *Fibers by the Yard* Sparkles decorative threads for tying at knees and elbows • Pink chalk or blush make-up for cheeks
INSTRUCTIONS: Follow general directions on page 20. • Tie thread around neck to make narrower head. • Make 3 buttons and 2 earrings from the Slice'n Bake designs. To make butterfly buttons, warm cane, then roll gently until diameter reduces. • Bake. Glue to ears and chest.

Adjusting the Cloth Doll Body

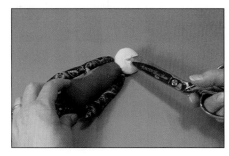

2. If the cloth head is too firm, the clay face will protrude too much. If needed, slit the front of the cloth head and remove some stuffing.

3. Pose doll. If legs and arms are too firm to bend, slit cloth behind elbows and knees and remove stuffing. With needle and thread, make a few stitches at hands, elbows, knees and/or feet to hold the doll in position.

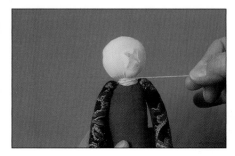

4. To make a narrower cloth head for use with narrower clay faces, wrap crochet thread tightly around the neck. Secure ends of thread.

Continued on pages 20 and 21.

Dolls with Cloth Bodies

Continued from pages 18 and 19.

GENERAL MATERIALS: *One & Only Creations* 12" Wild Woman doll • Cardboard for making pom poms • Make-up blush, chalk or Pearl-Ex for cheeks • Burnt Umber or Gold paint for antiquing face • Scissors • Hemostat • Needle • Thread • *Fabri-Tac* • *The Ultimate!* (for gluing face to cloth head)

Flaming Sun Doll

MATERIALS: *AMACO (*Sun Push Mold; Yellow polymer clay for face) • *Fibers By The Yard* Yellow yarn for hair • Pink chalk or blush make-up for cheeks • 24 gauge *Artistic Wire* (Copper, Magenta)
INSTRUCTIONS: Follow general directions. • Wrap the decorative wires around the body and face. Curl ends.

Jumping Rope Doll

MATERIALS: *AMACO* (Push Molds: Sun, Moon; Yellow polymer clay) • Assorted beads (8 Green bugle, 17 Yellow 1/8" clay, 18 frosted or plain Yellow glass E) • 15" Tinned Copper *Artistic Wire* 24 gauge • Ochre acrylic paint • Cream thread • Needle • Sponge • *The Ultimate!* glue
INSTRUCTIONS: Follow general directions. • Make 8 stars from Moon mold. Pierce holes in clay stars before baking, piercing hole front to back in 1 star and side to side in the other 7. • Paint cloth head with Ochre acrylic paint. Glue clay face over painted head. • String beads onto wire. Curl wire ends. • Sew cloth hands shut around ends of wire. • Make necklace using 8th star and thread. Tie around neck.

Moon Maiden Doll

MATERIALS: *AMACO* (Moon Push Mold; Yellow polymer clay) • *Fibers By The Yard* Green Garden yarn • Ribbon rose • Leaf • Beads for 6" necklace • 7" square Purple suede • Gold *Lumiere* paint • Cream thread • Needle • Sponge • *The Ultimate!* glue
INSTRUCTIONS: Follow general directions. • Paint face with Gold paint and rub on blush. • String beads on thread and tie around neck. • Fold over 1" on top edge of suede, then tie around waist. Sew tie ends in place. • Glue ribbon rose and leaf to side of head. • **Ribbon rose**: Fold 12" of 2" wide ribbon in half to make a long narrow strip. Loosely roll the ribbon, stitching bottom edge together every few inches as you roll. Make leaf by gathering ribbon. Tuck around the rose.

Shy Dancer

MATERIALS: *AMACO (*Sun Push Mold; Pale Lilac polymer clay for face) • *One & Only Creations* Sparkle yarn for hair • Purple paint for shoes • *Hanah* Silk ribbon (3 yards Cabernet 11/2" wide, 2 yards Green Apple 1" wide) • Pearl-Ex Pigments (Gold, Pink, Blue)
INSTRUCTIONS: Follow general directions, using large sun face without the rays. Brush face with Gold, Pink and Blue Pearl-Ex before baking. • Cut Cabernet ribbon into 12 pieces 8" long and one 12" piece. • Make a pom pom for 31/2" long hair. Do not cut loops. Glue hair to head. Tie bow around hair using 12" ribbon. • Cut Green ribbon into 10 pieces 31/2" long, 1 piece 6", and 1 piece 30". • Tie 12 Cabernet ribbon pieces to the long Green ribbon and 10 short Green pieces to the 6" Green ribbon, using a Lark's Head knot. • Clip the ends of the Green ribbon pieces to make slight fringe. Tie strung ribbons around neck and waist ending in a bow.

Making a Rag or Ribbon Fringe Skirt

1. Tie 12 Cabernet pieces to a 30" Green Apple ribbon using a Lark's Head knot. (Lay folded Cabernet ribbon over the long Green ribbon. Bring two cut ends of Cabernet ribbon under Green ribbon and through Cabernet loop. Pull the ends tight.)

Making Yarn and Fibers Hair

1. To make pom poms for hair, cut a piece of cardboard that is as wide as hair will be long. Tape a 5" piece of yarn over top of cardboard. • Wrap yarn around cardboard from 10 to 40 times, depending on thickness of yarn and desired fullness of hair.

2. Untape top piece of yarn and tie tightly over middle of wrapped yarn. Cut opposite side of wrapped yarn. Glue hair in place. Generally you will need 4 pom poms: one for the back of head, one on each side and one on top. The number needed depends greatly on the thickness of the yarn. Adjust as needed to fit your doll.

Continued on pages 22 and 23.

Bendi Dolls

GENERAL MATERIALS: *AMACO* (Sun Push Mold; What a Character Push Molds: #18 Boot; #12 Hands; Polymer clay: Yellow, White, Blue, Raspberry) • *Wimpole Street Creations* 15" cloth Bendi-doll • Pink make-up blush • Size 11 Yellow beads • 3¹/₂" wood skewer or wire • Ochre acrylic paint • *Tulip* Cool Color Spray paint (Lemon Peel, Petunia, Caribbean Blue) • Powder or cornstarch • Hemostat • Sewing (needle, thread, scissors) • Beading (needle, thread) • *Fabri-Tac* glue • *The Ultimate!* glue

Spring Sunshine Female Doll

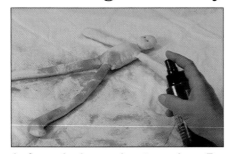

MATERIALS: *Hanah* Silk ribbon (3 yards Rose Nectar 1¹/₂" wide, 30" Green Apple 1" wide) • Silk Flowers with 30 small 4-petal sections that can be pulled apart

INSTRUCTIONS: Separate the silk flowers and glue petals to doll's head using *Fabri-Tac*. Cover back and all sides of head. Cut the Rose Nectar ribbon into 12 pieces 8" long. Wrap one piece tightly around waist and sew in place. Tie the other pieces to long Green ribbon, using Lark's Head knots. Tie around the waist ending in a bow. See Shy Dancer, page 20 for more details. Directions for finishing arms and legs are on page 22.

Sun Male Doll

MATERIALS: 2" circle of muslin to dye along with body and sew over back of head • 3 buttons • 8" ribbon 2" wide

Creating Doll Body & Face

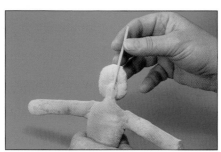

1. Spray body, overlapping colors. For male doll, spray a circle of fabric for covering back of head. Let dry.

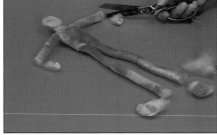

2. Cut off the tips of arms and 1" from each leg, avoiding wires. Pull out the excess stuffing.

Bendi Dolls are reworked and embellished with flower petals, ribbons, faces and boots.

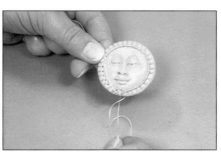

3. To stabilize the neck, slit back of neck and insert a wire or skewer piece. Stitch in place to secure.

4. Make large sun face. Pierce holes every ¹/₄" around face. Bake. Cool. Antique. String beads onto the thread. Lay string of beads around face. Tack string through holes in face. Hide knots behind the face.

5. Sew face to head. On male Sun Doll, sew a square of dyed fabric over the back of head to hide the stitches.

Bendi Dolls

These dolls are stepping out in style. Their flamboyant, multi-colored clay shoes are the "piece de resistance" of this project. Also note the marvelous effect from adding beads and flower petals around the face.

Creating Doll Hand with Arm and Skinner Blend Boots

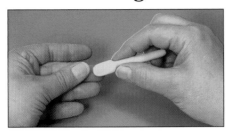

6. Hands: For each doll, roll two 3/4" balls of clay. Roll each into a rope. Flatten the ends slightly to make a paddle.

7. Press paddle into powdered mold. If you do not have a hand mold, leave hand paddle-shaped as in #6.

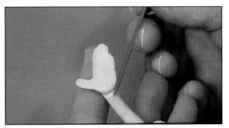

8. Define the wrist by rolling knitting needle around the back of wrist.

9. Press the needle across the middle of the palm.

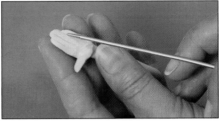

10. Use the needle to draw and press in the finger lines on palm side of hand.

11. Bend the hand as desired. Wrap and press a small rope of clay around the arm and bake.

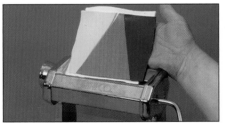

12. Skinner Blend for 2 Shoes (double for 4 shoes): Flatten Raspberry, Blue, Yellow and White clay at the thickest setting on the pasta machine. From White, cut a 4" x 5 1/2" rectangle. See photo. Cut Yellow, Raspberry and Blue triangles to cover White sheet. Run through pasta machine at the thickest setting. Fold sheet in half so the Yellow edge lays on top of Yellow edge and Blue lays on top of Blue edge.

With fold at the bottom, run through machine about 20 times, folding it exactly the same way each time. (For more instruction on doing a Skinner blend, see project # 1 - Moon Cupboard, page 28.)

13. Cut the resulting sheet in half. Stack. (Note: If you doubled the amount of clay to make 4 boots, cut stack in half again and save half for the second pair of

boots.) Flip stack 1/4 turn. Now the yellow is at the bottom. Run through the pasta machine at the thickest setting, yellow end first. Repeat at the middle setting and at one of the thinnest settings.

14. Accordion fold the long sheet of clay in 1" folds. Press against all sides of this stack to create a 3" long log.

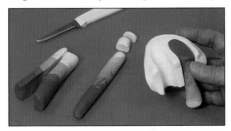

15. Cut log in half for boot. Press log into mold, bending clay around corner of mold to create heel.

16. Use leftover clay and boot mold to make inset lace piece and sole. Use round tool to press 3/4 way into boot. Roll to open a hole in center of boot. Pull and roll clay toes of boot to elongate and shape boot. Bake boots.

17. Antique boots. Wrap end of leg with thread, then glue into boots.

Little Stuffed Muslin Dolls

paint, draw and add personality with clay faces and pom pom hair

Let your imagination run wild as you paint or draw your unique designs on these muslin dolls. Clay faces and hair give each figure its own personality.

GENERAL MATERIALS: Permanent markers and/or fabric pens • Acrylic paint • Make-up blush • *Tulip* Cool Color Spray (Lemon Peel, Petunia, Caribbean Blue) • *Fabri-Tac* • *The Ultimate!* glue

GENERAL INSTRUCTIONS: Paint or dye bodies. • Make and bake clay heads. • Antique and add blush to cheeks. • Glue or sew heads in place. • Add words. • Make pom poms for hair. Glue in place. Let dry. Trim hair. • If hair sticks up, wet hair and let dry overnight.

Love/Rest/Peace Doll
Skip/Hop/Play Doll

MATERIALS: *AMACO* (Tribal Push Mold; Polymer clay: Gold, Ivory) • 3" muslin doll • Acrylic paint • Assorted yarns and ribbons

Flowers/Plant/Garden Doll
Initial Doll

MATERIALS: *AMACO* (Sun Push Mold; Yellow polymer clay) • 5" muslin doll • Acrylic paint • Yellow crochet cotton for Initial doll

Friend/Mentor Doll

MATERIALS: *AMACO* (Sun Push Mold; Yellow polymer clay) • 7" wired muslin doll • Spray dye (Yellow, Blue, Pink) • Green yarn

INSTRUCTIONS: Spray bodies with dye. Let dry. Make and bake clay head. Antique and add blush to cheeks. Glue or sew head in place. Draw designs and words. Dot on accents with markers or acrylic paints, using dotting technique on page 5. Make pom poms for hair and glue them in place.

Wake Up Doll

MATERIALS: *AMACO* (Victorian Push Mold; Ivory mix polymer clay, see page 7) • 7" wired muslin doll • Spray dye (Yellow, Blue, Pink) • Yellow crochet cotton

INSTRUCTIONS: Spray body with dye. Let dry. Make and bake clay head. Antique and add blush to cheeks. Glue or sew head in place. Draw designs and words. Dot on accents with markers or acrylic paints, using dotting technique on page 5. Make pom poms for hair and glue in place. Since crochet cotton is quite thin, you may need to make many small pom poms in order to fill head. When glue is dry, trim hair. If the hair sticks up, wet the hair and let dry overnight.

Fly a Kite Doll

MATERIALS: *AMACO* (Sun Push Mold; Ivory mix polymer clay, see page 7) • 7" wired muslin doll • *Fibers By The Yard* Beyond Black yarn

INSTRUCTIONS: Make and bake clay head. Antique and add blush to cheeks. Glue or sew head in place. Draw designs and words. Dot on accents with markers or acrylic paints. Make pom poms for hair and glue in place.

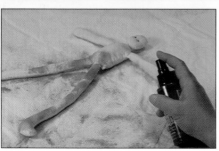

1. Spray body, overlapping the colors. Let dry.

Wrapped Dolls to Wear

folk art inspired dolls add interest to your wardrobe

Make these wonderful dolls to wear as pins. The fabric stuffed body acts as a base to wrap fabric strips. Add a molded face and wrap the body with layers of yarn, string and thread strung with beads. Sew hair in place, add buttons, more beads and charms along with a pin clasp on the back.

GENERAL MATERIALS: Fabric for body • Stuffing • Fabric, yarn, string for wrapping body • Assorted beads and charms • Burnt Umber acrylic paint for antiquing face • Pink make-up blush • Sewing (Scissors, Needle, Thread) • Beading (Needle, Thread) • Pin back

Lavender Dragonfly Doll
MATERIALS: *AMACO* (Victorian Push Mold; Copper polymer clay) • Dragonfly charm • Assorted beads

Purple Power Doll
MATERIALS: *AMACO* (Sun Push Mold; Violet polymer clay) • Freshwater pearls

Sleeping In Peace
MATERIALS: *AMACO* (Victorian Push Mold; Pink Flesh polymer clay) • Unraveled fabric

General Instructions for Doll

1. Cut 2 pattern pieces from fabric. Sew seam, leaving hole for turning. Turn. Stuff.

2. Cut 1" wide strips of fabric to wrap doll. Wrap tightly. Sew in place.

3. Make and bake the clay face. Sew or glue to body. Wrap body with layers of yarn, string, thread and/or strung beads.

4. Sew hair in place. Cut to desired lengths and knot

pieces together to hold. Leave some pieces longer for braiding or wrapping with contrasting threads. Add beads, buttons and charms. Sew pin finding on back.

Large Masked Figure

MATERIALS: *AMACO* (Sun Push Mold; Polymer clay: Yellow, Violet) • Poseable Wood Figure • Acrylic paint (Olive, Rust, Ochre) • 24 gauge Copper wire • Toothpick

Small Masked Figure

MATERIALS: *AMACO* (Sun Push Mold; White polymer clay) • Poseable Wood Figure • *Lumiere* paint (Super Copper, Metallic Olive Green, Pearl Violet) • String for mask

1. Paint the figure. Leave all of the joints unpainted. Drill a hole in each toe for toothpick.

2. To make mask, don't completely fill face mold. While face is still in mold, use thumb to make back of face concave. Pierce face with one hole at each side for string. Bake over foil ball.

3. Large figure necklace and shoes: Roll 8 Yellow 1/4" balls, 2 Violet 1/3" balls and 7 purple pepper-shaped beads from polymer clay. Press piece of toothpick into Violet balls. Pierce others for stringing. Bake. Press Violet balls onto shoes. String on 8" piece of wire. Wrap around neck, curling wire ends behind head.

4. Antique mask. Rub blush onto cheeks. Thread wire through holes in mask with ends in front. Fit to head, then trim, leaving 1/2" on each end. Curl ends.

Poseable Wood Dolls

Clay masks and accents bring these wood figures to life. Notice the balls on the toes of the shoes and the clay necklace.

Painted Wood

Turn a plain set of wood drawers into a beautiful work of art with a bit of paint and a small amount of clay. The drawer pulls are made from small clay balls. The face and other shapes are made from easy-to-use molds.

Dressing the Cupboard

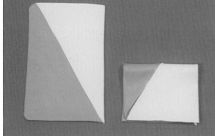

1. Roll Yellow and White clay at thickest setting of pasta machine. Cut a 5" tall x 3" wide right triangle from each color. Flip the White one and layer as in photo. Fold in half.

2. With fold at the bottom, run through machine. • Fold again and repeat, being sure that White is folded on White edge and Yellow on Yellow edge.

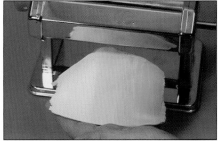

3. Repeat 20 times, folding it exactly the same each time, creating a gradated sheet. Rotate sheet 1/4 turn so White is on bottom.

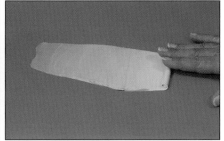

With pasta machine at middle setting, run sheet through with White edge first. Repeat with smaller setting. **4.** Starting with the White edge, tightly roll the sheet into a rope.

5. Firmly squeeze resulting rope of colored clay to force out air bubbles, carefully keeping the rope round. Roll to reduce rope to 1/2" in diameter. Slice five 1/2" pieces.

6. Paint the cupboard with 1-2 coats of Blue paint. Trim with White paint that is tinted Blue.

7. Pound a nail into the center of each drawer to hold knob.

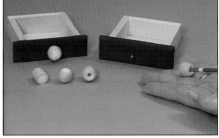

8. To make knobs, roll clay chunks into balls. Fit clay over nail. Remove knob and bake. Glue knob in place.

Moon Cupboard

MATERIALS: *AMACO* (Moon Push Mold; Polymer clay: Yellow, White, Pale Blue) • *Kalco Krafts* 5 mini drawer wood box KC505 • Acrylic paint (Blue, Yellow, White) • Make-up blush or chalk • 1/2"- 3/4" nails • Hammer • Sandpaper • *The Ultimate!* glue

INSTRUCTIONS: Paint cupboard Blue. Paint trim Light Blue. Let dry. • Pound nails into center of each drawer. • Make knobs from a Skinner Blend of Yellow and White clay. • Use leftover Skinner Blend for stars and face. See photo. • Make words from Pale Blue clay. • Bake all clay pieces. • Paint words Dark Blue. Let dry. Lightly sand word surface to create contrast. • Antique face lightly with Blue paint. Dry brush with White and Yellow paint for highlights. Rub blush on cheeks. • Glue all clay pieces in place.

Game Pieces and Little Gifts

The Sun
MATERIALS: *AMACO* (Sun Push Mold; Yellow polymer clay) • Tall spool • Acrylic paint (Plum, Lavender, Lime) • Round toothpick
INSTRUCTIONS: Paint spool. See photo. • Roll two $1/2$" balls of Yellow clay. Roll 1 into a rope and press into top of spool. Press toothpick through rope, into spool, to hold clay in place. Press face to front of rope. • Bake. • Glue clay to spool. • Antique face

Half Moon
MATERIALS: *AMACO* (Moon Push Mold; Yellow polymer clay) • Tall spool • Acrylic paint (Plum, Lavender, Teal) • 12" Clear Green *Fun Wire* 24 gauge • Leftover Skinner Blend cane slices from Spring Sunshine doll
INSTRUCTIONS: Paint spool. Make dots using dot technique on page 5. • Press a $1/2$" ball of Yellow clay over top of spool. Decorate edge with slices from the Skinner Blend cane. • Roll a $3/4$" Yellow ball into a short rope. Insert toothpick into rope. Press into top of spool. Make clay face and press over rope. Make clay star and press to tip of moon. • Cut 3" pieces of wire. Curl with pliers or around knitting needle. Press wires into clay. • Bake. • Antique.

The Crowned King
MATERIALS: *AMACO* (Tribal Push Mold; Polymer clay: Yellow, Blue, Raspberry) • Tall spool • 7 straight pins • Acrylic paint (Ochre, Yellow, Green) • 8" Non-Tarnish Silver *Artistic Wire* 24 gauge • *The Ultimate!* glue
INSTRUCTIONS: **Spool**: Paint spool. See photo. Make dots using dot technique. See page 5. • Roll a $3/4$" ball of Yellow clay into a $11/2$" rope. Insert toothpick into rope. • Make face and press to front of rope. • Add a $1/3$" ball of Blue clay for neck. • Press into spool to check fit. Then remove. • **Crown**: Roll seven $1/8$" Raspberry balls. Press balls over heads of pins. Stick pins into top of head. • **Hands**: Roll two $1/4$" Yellow balls. • **Arms**: Roll a $3/4$" ball of Blue clay into a short chunk. • Press thin knitting needle or rod into center of chunk. Roll, then stretch chunk until desired diameter is achieved. Measure two $11/2$" pieces. Remove extra clay from rod. Rotate clay to make sure that it will come off rod after baking. Bake all clay pieces. Glue head to spool. • Clay may be baked in one long tube shape, then cut with a very sharp clay slicing blade while it is still warm. • **Assemble arms**: Form a loop at the end of wire. Add, in this order, one hand, arm, arm, second hand, leaving a 2" space between the arms. With space at back of neck, wrap wire around neck once, readjusting arms as needed. Trim wire to fit, then form loop at other end of wire to hold arms in place.

The Diva Queen
MATERIALS: *AMACO* (Tribal Push Mold; Polymer clay: Yellow, Blue, Raspberry, Lime) • Straight clothespin • Clothespin base • 5 straight pins • 2 glass beads for hands • Acrylic paint (Ochre, Yellow, Green) • 8" Non-Tarnish Silver *Artistic Wire* 24 gauge
INSTRUCTIONS: See directions for The King. • Press ball of clay over top of clothespin to form back of head. • Press face to clay-covered "head". • Wrap a strip of clay around face for hood.

Game Pieces and Little Gifts
made from wood spools, clothespins, and molded polymer clay

Game Pieces

GENERAL MATERIALS: Acrylic paint (Burnt Umber, Ochre) • Wire cutters • Round-nose pliers • Polymer Clay Blade • Make-up blush or Pink chalk • *The Ultimate!* glue

Making the King

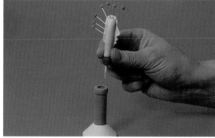

1. Press head into spool to check fit.

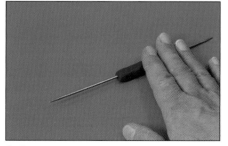

2. Press thin knitting needle or rod into center of chunk. Roll.

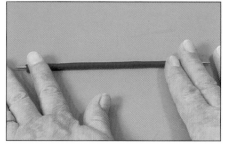

3. Continue to roll and stretch chunk until desired diameter is achieved. Measure two 1¹/₂" pieces. Remove extra clay from rod. Rotate clay to make sure that it will come off rod after baking. Bake all clay pieces.

Games aren't just for kids. More and more adults are gathering for "game night" and considerable effort is being invested in decorating these game rooms. Add a special touch to your game table with these game pieces.

Wired

MATERIALS: *AMACO* (Sun Push Mold; Yellow polymer clay; 21" Clear Blue *Fun Wire* 24 gauge) • Wood spool • Leftover Skinner Blend cane slices from Spring Sunshine doll • 3 round toothpicks

INSTRUCTIONS: **Spool:** Press 1 slice of Skinner Blend cane, 1" wide and ¹/₂" thick, over top of spool. Reduce another piece of cane to ¹/₄" diameter. Cut slices and press around edge of spool. • **Body:** Roll two ¹/₂" Yellow clay balls. Make face from one. Flatten the other slightly and press face over it. Insert onto toothpick. Add small clay ball for neck. Press into slice of cane for body. Press toothpick with body and head into top of spool. Cut and curl 6 wires, each 3" long. Press into head. • **Hands:** Roll two ¹/₄" balls of Yellow clay. Press over ends of toothpicks. Press toothpicks into body. Bake. Antique clay.

Moon Magic

MATERIALS: *AMACO* (Moon Push Mold; Polymer clay: Yellow, Blue, Gold) • Cane slice and clay scraps left from Moon Cupboard • Wood spool • 18" Non-Tarnish Silver *Artistic Wire* • Round toothpick

INSTRUCTIONS: Roll two ³/₄" balls of clay, one Blue and one Yellow. • Flatten Blue ball. • Make face from Yellow one. • Cut wire into 7 pieces 2¹/₂" long. • Curl with pliers. • Press onto Blue circle. • For neck, roll a ¹/₄" ball of Gold clay. Press onto toothpick. Lay over Blue circle. Press on face. Bake clay pieces. • Cut 2 slices from leftover Moon Cupboard cane. Press 1 slice flat onto spool and the other upright on spool. Press toothpick with face into center of spool. • Bake. • Antique face. • Glue clay to spool.

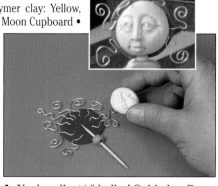

1. Neck: roll a ¹/₄" ball of Gold clay. Press onto toothpick. Lay over Blue circle. Press on face. Bake.

Art with Found Objects
imaginative, one-of-a-kind art dolls

Use found objects to make creative, imaginative, one-of-a-kind art dolls. Dominoes, old boxes, keys, tags and spoons were used in making our dolls. However, you will find your own great treasures to use.

These projects will hopefully give you some ideas to expand on to make your own fabulous Found Object Art Dolls!

GENERAL MATERIALS: Make-up blush, chalk or Pearl-Ex • Burnt Umber or Gold paint • Scissors • Wire cutters • Needle-nose pliers • Flat-nose pliers • Drill • *The Ultimate!* glue

GENERAL INSTRUCTIONS: Determine where face will be, and how to attach it. If possible, add face with wire or stick to preserve integrity of found item. • Age added pieces with paint to match found item.

Office Madonna Staples Box
MATERIALS: *AMACO* (Sun Push Mold; White polymer clay) • Metal rimmed tag • Wood skewer • 2 keys • Burnt Umber acrylic paint • *Lumiere* paint (Pearl White, Metallic Gold) • *Krylon* Gold Leafing pen • Rubber band • 18 gauge steel wire • 1/2 cup of small stones • Antique box

INSTRUCTIONS: Bake face. • Paint and antique face and tag. • Punch hole in top of box. Cut skewer to fit box. Glue face and tag to skewer. Let dry. • Fill box 1/4 full of stones. Place rubber band around bottom to hold box closed. • Insert skewer with head into box. Wrap wire around neck, then drape over sides and through keys.

Morning Cocoa
MATERIALS: *AMACO* (Sun Push Mold; Pale Brown polymer clay) • Antique can • 2 measuring spoons • 24-26 gauge Copper wire • *Lumiere* Metallic Gold paint • Acrylic paint (Burnt Umber, White) • Metal paint (Green, Rust)

INSTRUCTIONS: See photos at left.

Turn Key Keeper
MATERIALS: *AMACO* (Sun Push Mold; Champagne polymer clay) • Steel wire (gauge: 20, 22, 28) • Heater key • Acrylic paint (Burnt Umber, Black)

INSTRUCTIONS: Bake face with holes for mask. • Curl a loop of wire and press ends into tool. • Wire face to tool. Glue as needed to keep face from shifting. • Wrap arm wire around neck. Curl ends. • Paint wire Black to match tool.

Domino Man
MATERIALS: *AMACO* (Tribal Push Mold; Gold polymer clay) • Domino • Wood skewer • 4 eye pins • Burnt Umber acrylic paint

INSTRUCTIONS: Press 1/2" Gold clay ball onto skewer. Press face over ball. • Make 1/8" thick rope arms. • Embed eye pin into each arm. Bake clay. • Drill hole in top of domino for wood skewer and into sides for eye pins. Insert eye pins and skewer into holes. Add glue. • Attach arms to eye pins.

Office Madonna

1. Glue face to tag, with skewer in between.

2. Sponge paint measuring spoons with metal paint to resemble colors of can.

Morning Cocoa

1. Press a 1 1/2" x 1/2" clay rope to index card. Lay 18" of wire over clay. Press face over wire. Bake.

3. Wrap face wire around can. Twist tightly at back of can. Thread spoons onto a second piece of wire. Twist wire at top of each spoon to hold them out from can. Wrap wire around can.

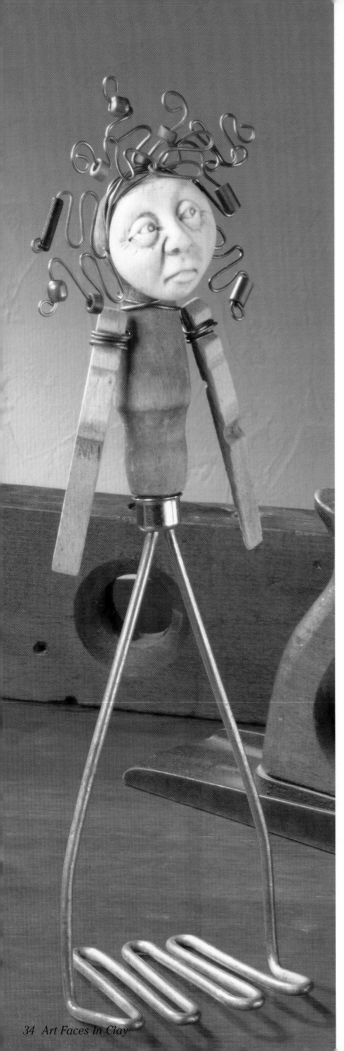

Potato Masher Art Doll

turn everyday objects into fun, whimsical art

Stretch your creative envelope with found objects. Doing so makes you look at everyday objects with "new" eyes.

Potato Masher Man

MATERIALS: *AMACO* (Moon Push Mold; White polymer clay) • Potato masher • Clip clothespin • 5-6 pieces 18" Steel wire 18 gauge • Burnt Umber acrylic paint • Assorted beads

Masher Art Doll

1. Glue the face to the head. Wrap one wire under head with ends on top.

2. Twist ends together once, then bend. Add beads, curling wire to secure.

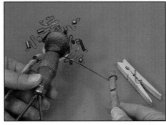

3. Take clothespin apart. If the clothespin is not aged, antique it to make it look old. Wrap wire around clothespin, then around neck, ending with other clothespin.

Punch Tool Guard Doll

Antique Punch Tool Guard Doll

MATERIALS: *AMACO* (Tribal Push Mold; Pale Brown polymer clay) • 2 keys • 18 gauge and 26 gauge steel wire • Burnt Umber acrylic paint • Bark pieces for hair • Antique punch
INSTRUCTIONS: Bake face with holes for mask. • Position bark between tool and face. Drill holes through bark. Wire face to bark and tool. Glue to keep bark from shifting. • Wrap wire around neck and through keys. Curl ends of wire. • Antique face.

Twig Tassel Doll

Twig Tassel Doll
MATERIALS: *AMACO* (Tribal Push Mold; Ivory mix polymer clay; *WireForm* Brass Decorative Mesh) • *Create A Tassel* Wood tassel topper 84928) • Acrylic paint (White, Burnt Umber, Black) • 18 gauge steel wire • 11 old nails (or new nails distressed to look old) • Brass washers • Dry Twigs

Making the Twig Tassel

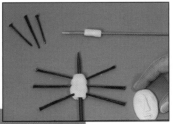

1. Paint tassel topper White.

2. Distress wood. Paint with Burnt Umber and wipe it off immediately. Rub Black on in places and wipe off. Add water if needed to blend colors and remove paint.

3. Roll a 1" ball of faux Ivory polymer clay. Elongate to oval shape. Press needle through center of oval, then flatten slightly. Press 6 nails into oval. Make face from faux Ivory clay.

Use a knife to cut shallow lines into molded face. Press the clay face over nails. Make a long clay bead for the neck. Bake all the clay pieces.

4. Unravel long wire strands from the Brass WireForm. Tie squares of WireForm and washers to the wire strands.

5. Bundle twigs along with wired washers and wired metal squares. Wrap top tightly with wire. Fold 18" of 18 gauge wire in half. Thread through top of twigs to act as a hanger. Add glue to top of twigs. Thread hanger into tassel topper.

6. Add neck washers, neck bead and head. Glue 3 more nails into hole at top of head, around hanger. Wrap unraveled WireForm wires around arm nails, and wrap around neck to secure.

Rag Tassel Doll
the perfect accent art

Hand-dyed fabrics coordinate well with the painted body and hair on this pretty rag tassel doll. The hand-painted details on the face are reminiscent of fine porcelain dolls. This feminine tassel would make a lovely addition to a little girl's room.

Rag Tassel Doll

MATERIALS: *AMACO* (Victorian Push Mold; Ivory mix polymer clay; White *Fun Wire* 18 gauge) • *Create A Tassel* Wood tassel topper 84927) • Acrylic paint (White, Yellow, Pink) • Paints and makeup blush for face • Fabric ripped in 1" x 18" strips • *Fibers By The Yard* Only Orange yarn • Hammer • Drill • Needle tools • Round-nose pliers • Flat-nose pliers • Wire cutters

Making Rag Body

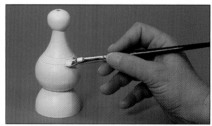

1. Paint wood topper White. Let dry. Wipe with Yellow paint on paper towel.

2. Use brush to paint Pink into grooves, immediately wipe with paper towel to stain rest of tassel topper.

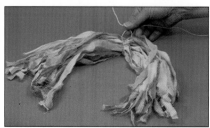

3. Gather strips of fabric together. Wrap wire around center. Thread the wires into tassel topper, then through body. Make head. Paint face before or after baking clay. Make hair as for pom poms. Glue to head. Wrap the braided fibers around neck. Leave the ends for arms.

Making the

1. Paint wood tassel topper Green. Dry brush highlights with Silver and Gold.

4. Mix faux jade polymer clay. Make the Sun Face. Press onto a 3/4" ball of clay. Press over skewer or knitting needle. Make a neck bead from faux Ivory polymer clay. See photo.

7. Cut a 15" piece of wire. Fold in half and put through two holes in the pierced disk.

10. Use the round-nose pliers to crimp loop.

Fork Tassel Doll

Found objects can be delightfully fun when made into tassels. Antique forks remind you of wind chimes.

Fork Tassel

MATERIALS: *AMACO* (Sun Push Mold; Ivory and Jade mix polymer clay) • *Create A Tassel* Wood tassel topper 84924 • 4 antique sliver forks • *Lumiere* paint (Metallic Olive Green, Metallic Silver, Metallic Gold) • *Artistic Wire* 18 gauge Non-Tarnish Silver • Assorted beads • Fishing line

Metal Fork Tassel Doll

2. Hammer the forks flat.

3. Drill a hole in the end of each fork.

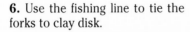

5. From leftover clay, make round disk to fit in center of tassel topper. Pierce 4 holes through the center. Press 4 grooves along the sides of disk. These grooves will keep the forks from shifting posi- tion once they are tied to the disk. Bake the disk, neck bead and face.

6. Use the fishing line to tie the forks to clay disk.

8. Thread wire through the tassel topper, neck bead and head.

9. Pull wire tightly so that the clay disk inside tassel topper does not rock. Fold both wires over round-nose pliers.

11. Use flat-nose pliers to wrap both wires tightly around the base of the loop. Trim the ends of wires. Tuck wire ends between the loop and the back of head. Finish by wrapping two 18" wires around the "waist". Thread on the beads. Bend and twist the wires into arm shapes following photo. Attach the fishing line as a hanger.

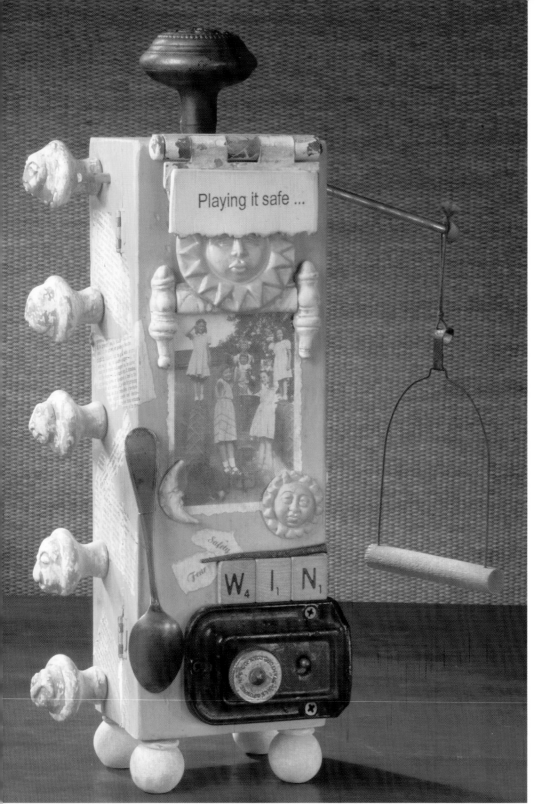

Playing it safe ...

W I N

Make fabulous, fun and unique hands-on art!

Making Your Own Molds

1. Rub powder or cornstarch over softened polymer clay. Press shape into clay. Remove carefully. Bake clay.

2. To use the molds, brush with powder. Fill mold, being careful to not overfill. Use second piece of clay to lift design from mold.

Creating the Story Box

1. Paint the box.

2. Make feet from balls of foil covered with polymer clay. Press tack on top of ball and cover with thin piece of clay.

3. Bake feet, then dry brush. Glue to bottom of box using *The Ultimate!* glue.

4. Collage the clippings, words, and torn paper to box using Collage Gel.

5. Attach knobs to side of box. Press faces made of air dry clay over knobs. **6.** To transfer words to clay, place photocopy (reverse copy of words) upside

Story Box

altered art in a box

Story boxes are part scrapbook, part journal, part altered book, and always creative. They are a terrific place for displaying themed collections. Best of all, it tells "your" story!

Playing It Safe

A general materials list is provided to give you an idea of the supplies used to complete this box. Adapt the list to fit your theme and collections.
Design Originals Collage paper #0547 Dictionary • AMACO (Push Molds: Sun, Tribal, Moon; Polymer clay: Yellow, White, Ivory, Green) • Hearty Clay Air dry clay • Walnut Hollow Candle Box 17020P • 4 thumbtacks • Bird cage swing • Lumiere Metallic Gold paint • Acrylic paint (Burnt Umber, White, Yellow, Green, Rust, Plum) • 5 Drawer knobs and screws • Decoupage Collage Gel • The Ultimate! glue

down on flat piece of clay. Burnish with bone folder or flat edge to ensure good contact between clay and paper. Bake, then remove paper.

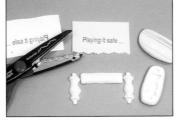

7. Trim baked, hot clay with scalloped scissors. Do not bend it. Hot clay is fragile. Make molding pieces using polymer clay and molds.

8. Glue all embellishments in place. Paint and antique pieces to blend with box.

9. Fill inside of box with framed pictures (purchased or made with polymer clay, etc.), collections, masks, dolls, beads.

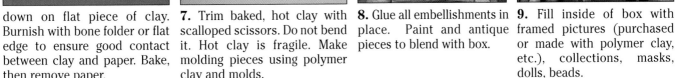

Mokume Gane Jewelry
from versatile polymer clay

Mokume Gane is a technique in which layers of metal are fused to create stripes or wood grain effects. This technique is easily adapted to clay. By stacking, cutting, and restacking clay, many interesting patterns emerge.

Tools: Needle tools • Round-nose pliers • Flat-nose pliers • Wire cutter • Burnt Umber acrylic paint • Wet/dry sandpaper (Grit: 220, 320, 400, 600) • Beading (Thread, Needle)

Red/Gold Man and Blue Man
MATERIALS: *AMACO* (Sun Push Mold; Polymer clay: Ivory mix, Bordeaux, Gold, White, Translucent Blue) • 9" Copper wire 22 gauge • Assorted beads (Tube, seed, "E")
INSTRUCTIONS: **Head**: Make a 1/2" diameter flat bead, using any color. Bake. • With baked bead on needle, press 1/2" flattened ball of clay to back of bead and face to front of bead. Blend seam with finger. Shape head. • The baked bead inside of head makes it easier to shape.• **Body**: Start with a 1" ball of clay. Save any pieces with Blue coloring for the Blue necklace. • Shape into a teardrop. Flatten slightly. Pierce a hole through center of bead. • Make small bead for neck. • Bake beads. • Sand and buff large bead. See page 51, step 2. • Thread wire through hole in bead body, then thread both ends through neck bead and head, making wire loop in top. • **Arms**: Thread a 20" length of beading thread onto beading needle. Tie end of thread to neck, leaving a tail. Starting at right shoulder, add beads following order of beads in photo. Thread needle back through next to last bead and continue through other beads until you reach neck again. Tie knot around neck. • Repeat with second arm. Knot thread. Hide ends in last few beads on string if possible. Add a drop of glue to knot. • With another length of beading thread, add extra beads around neck for collar and to help shape shoulders. • **Hair**: For Blue Mokume Gane Man, make beaded strands for hair the same as for arms, except tie threads to top wire loop. Hide thread ends in beads. • For Red/Gold Man, make loops instead of strands by going through each bead only once, then tying end of strand to top loop.

Mokume Gane Variation
This variation uses a Victorian face with Red, Blue, Gold, Translucent and White for the Mokume Gane layers.

How to Make Mokume Gane

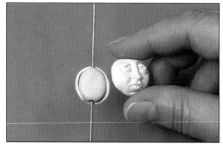

1. Press face to front of baked bead.

2. Flatten conditioned clay, except for face and bottom layer of clay to 1/16" thick (use thickest setting of pasta machine). Cut a 2" x 2" square of each

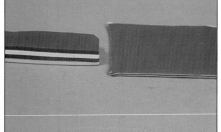

color except for bottom layer. Stack. • Roll stack through pasta machine at thickest setting. • Cut in half. Stack and roll again. • Repeat one more time. Stack.

3. Condition another color of clay to use as a bottom "cushion" layer. Press cushion, cut the same size as the stack, to table in front of you. Lay stacked clay onto cushion. Press interesting shapes into top of clay, pushing hard enough to go into cushion.

4. Use sharp blade to slice thin pieces off top of stack.

5. Roll a ball of clay the desired size of bead. Press slices onto bead.

6. Roll bead to smooth slices. Shape bead into desired shape.

Designer Push Molds

Flexible Molds for Easy Release

Moon Mold Shapes

Turn your finished molded pieces and shapes from ordinary into extraordinary art pieces.

Victorian Mold Shapes

To finish molds :
· Antique
· Paint
· Change Expressions
· Stretch
· Use Part of Mold
· Add Details
· Compress
· Change Shape

Molds for Creating Wonderful Faces and Themed Words

Sun Mold Shapes

Use with:
- Polymer Clays
- Plaster of Paris
- Air Dry, Non-Dry Modeling Clays
- Craft Soap Candle Wax

Sunshine

Sky

Light

Warmth

Turn Molds into works of art with color.
See page 7 for making Faux Marble,
Jade and Ivory

Tribal Mold Shapes

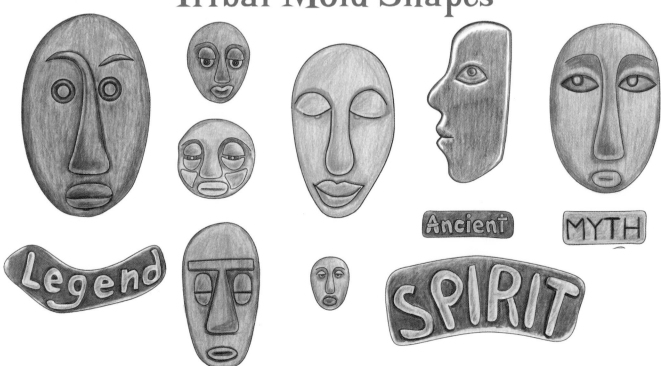

Legend

Ancient

MYTH

SPIRIT

Little Wish Book

write down your dreams and goals on these pages

Moon Book

MATERIALS: *AMACO* (Moon Push Mold; Polymer clay: Blue, Yellow, White) • Brown acrylic paint • 10" Non-Tarnish Silver *Artistic Wire* 24 gauge • White cardstock or book cloth • White paper • *Krylon* Gold Metallic marker • *The Ultimate!* glue

INSTRUCTIONS: **Clay**: Condition clay. • Mix White with Yellow to make Pale Yellow clay for moon and word. • Roll Blue clay to 1/16" thick. • Use deckle scissors to cut 2 pieces 2" x 2¹/2" long for book covers. • Texture clay with fabric. Press moon and word to front cover. Make a 2¹/2" long tube bead from Blue clay. • Bake all clay pieces. • Antique the Yellow pieces. • **Assemble covers**: Lay front and back cover side by side. Cut cardstock or book cloth to fit across both clay pieces. Glue. • **Wire**: Thread wire through tube bead, around inside of cover, then back through other end of tube bead. Pull wire taut, being careful not to rip paper. Curl wire ends. • **Pages**: Cut pages to fit book and slide under inside wire. • Edge pieces with Gold marker.

Push molds -
Easy !
Fun !
Fast !

1. Lay front and back cover side by side. Cut cardstock or book cloth to fit across both clay pieces. Glue.

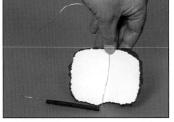

2. Thread wire through tube bead, around inside of cover, then back through other end of tube bead. Pull wire taut, being careful not to rip paper.

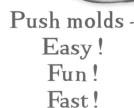

3. Curl wire ends.

4. Cut pages to fit book and slide under inside wire.

Making Collage Book Cover

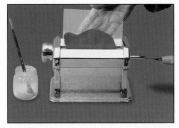

1. To create texture, roll powdered, flattened clay through a pasta machine with a texture sheet.

2. To create charms, embed bent eye pin between two duplicate faces or words.

3. Sponge the baked collage pieces with paint to create color variations.

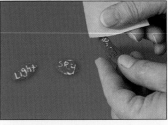

4. Lightly sand the top of words to remove paint and reveal Yellow clay.

5. Glue collage together, then drill holes for beading.

Morning Journal: My Book of Wishes

MATERIALS: *AMACO* (Sun Push Mold; One block each Polymer clay: Yellow, White, Blue) • 4¼" x 6¼" Journal • Acrylic paint (Yellow, Brown, Pale Blue, Navy, Green, Purple) • 3 eye pins • *Krylon* Gold Metallic marker • Silver 20 gauge wire • White seed beads • Beading (Needle, White thread) • Decorative threads for tassel • 2 pieces cardstock cut to size of cover • *The Ultimate!* glue

INSTRUCTIONS: **Clay:** Condition clay. Mix pale colors by adding White clay to ½ of Blue and ½ of Yellow clay. • Use mold and Pale Yellow clay to make 1 large face, 2 tiny faces, 2 sunshine and 1 each of "light", "sky" and "warmth". • Thread slightly bent eye pin into top of both tiny faces and between sandwiched sunshine pieces. • Roll Pale Blue and Blue clay to ¹/16" thick. Tear or cut pieces for sky, 2 clouds, 2 ponds, a mountain and a river. Arrange pieces on cardstock, adjusting sizes as needed. Don't press together. • Brush each piece lightly with cornstarch, then add texture to pieces by rolling through pasta machine with texture sheets or by pressing with paper towel or fabric to represent sky, forests and water. • Bake all pieces. • **Paint:** With damp sponge, lightly tap watered down Light Blue, Blue and Yellow paint onto Pale Blue pieces. Paint top of mountain Purple and bottom Green. Wipe off paint, leaving color in recesses. Lightly antique the charms and large face. Paint words Blue. Let dry. Sand lightly over words to reveal Yellow clay. • Outline edges of large sun with Gold marker. • Lay out pieces on cardstock and glue together. Let dry. • **Drill:** Drill holes for beads. • **Sew:** Thread beading needle. Knot thread. Glue knot to back of clay. Starting at top of sun, on back side, put needle through hole, pick up a bead, then go back through same hole. • Continue to next hole, repeating steps. • At end, tie knot and glue. • Glue clay pieces to cover. • **Drill:** Drill 4 holes in each corner of collage, through clay and cover, for wires. Thread wires through 2 corner holes. Use beading thread to secure ends in place. Use round-nose pliers to curl ends. • **Finish:** Cut cardstock to fit inside cover. Glue in place to cover threads. • String tiny faces and sunshine onto threads. Make tassel, adding words. Glue tassel end to inside back cover.

General Tools: Beading (Thread, Needle) • Deckle scissors • Texture sheets or fabric • Drill • Drill bit smaller diameter than beads • Sandpaper • Paper towels • Wire cutters • Round-nose pliers • Sponge • *The Ultimate!* glue

Clay Collage Book Cover

Seed beads add another dimension to molded and textured clay. Arrange the elements and colors to suit your personality in this exciting free-form collage.

6. Add seed beads, sewing through collage.

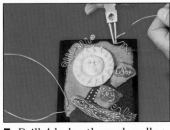

7. Drill 4 holes through collage and book cover. Thread wires through and curl.

8. Make tassel. Thread charms onto separate 20" threads. Tie together with tassel.

9. Secure the wire ends with beading thread, then tie on inside cover.

Photo Album Cover

With clay, you can make a frame any size you want. This one offers an ivy vine of beautiful flowers and leaves. Reminiscent of Victorian garden statuary, clay faces complete the composition with classical flair.

Using simple techniques, you can turn the same clay faces into attractive pins with delicate flowers.

1. Sponge paint album cover, one color at a time, overlapping and blending colors. Highlight with White and Gold paint.

2. Roll a 1/2" thick rope of Yellow clay. Flatten and cut 4 pieces to frame photo. Lay frame on paper. • Roll a skinny Green rope for a vine and lay around frame. Use molds to make flowers and leaves, faces and hearts. Press to frame. • Burnish photocopy of words to clay. • Bake clay pieces. • Add flowers and face to word piece. Bake word piece a second time.

Victorian Scrapbook

MATERIALS: *AMACO* (Victorian Push Mold; Polymer clay: Leaf Green, Pink, White, Yellow, Violet; Designer Molds: Violet and Ivy 12227D, Hearts and Swirls 12226C, Pansies 12224A) • Scrapbook • Acrylic paint (White, Yellow, Metallic Olive, Metallic Gold) • Decorative thread, lace, string or yarn • Photocopy of words (reverse copy) • *Decoupage and Collage Gel* • *The Ultimate!* glue

INSTRUCTIONS: Sponge paint album cover, one color at a time, overlapping and blending colors. Highlight with White and Gold. • Condition clay to desired color. Roll a 1/2" thick rope of Yellow clay. Flatten and cut 4 pieces to frame photo. Lay frame on paper. • Roll a skinny Green rope for a vine and lay around frame. Use molds to make flowers and leaves, faces and hearts. Press to frame. • Burnish photocopy of words to clay. • Bake clay pieces. • Add flowers and face to word piece. Bake word piece a second time. • Dry brush White paint onto baked clay. Glue photo to front of album. Glue frame and word piece in place. Add lace trim and yarn.

Victorian Pins

MATERIALS: *AMACO* (Victorian Push Mold; Polymer clay: Leaf Green, Pink, White, Yellow, Blue) • Acrylic paint (White, Pink, Light Brown) • 1/2" pin back • *Super Glue*

INSTRUCTIONS: Condition clay and mix colors. • Flatten a 1/3" ball of White clay to a piece of paper. Make face and press to flattened ball. • Make tiny floral shapes, leaves, ribbons and hair from clay and press to face. • Bake. • Paint face. • Dry brush lightly with White paint to antique. • Glue on pin back.

Making roses: Flatten a rope of clay. Roll up lightly. Squeeze bottom edge together. Feather out top edge with finger. • **Leaves**: Roll a ball, then roll on one side to create a teardrop shape. Flatten. Press center with needle tool to make line. • **Ball Flowers**: Roll tiny ball. Press in place, then press center with rounded brush handle. • **Hair**: Flatten a rope of clay. Press with needle tool or end of knife to make hair lines. • **Ruffle**: Flatten a rope of clay. Press with a rounded tool to make indentations.